My First DINOSAUR Book

Clive Gifford

WINDMILL BOOKS™

New York

Published in 2023 by **Windmill Books**,
an Imprint of Rosen Publishing,
29 East 21st Street, New York, NY 10010

Copyright © 2020 Miles Kelly Publishing Ltd

Cataloging-in-Publication Data
Names: Gifford, Clive.
Title: My first dinosaur book / Clive Gifford.
Description: New York : Windmill Books, 2023. | Series: My first facts
Identifiers: ISBN 9781508198772 (pbk.) | ISBN 9781508198789 (library bound) | ISBN 9781508198796 (ebook)
Subjects: LCSH: Dinosaurs--Juvenile literature.
Classification: LCC QE861.5 G437 2023 | DDC 567.9--dc23

Manufactured in the United States of America
CPSIA Compliance Information: Batch CSWM23: For Further Information contact Rosen Publishing, New York, New York at 1-800-237-9932

Find us on

My First Facts

My FIRST DINOSAUR Book

Clive Gifford

WINDMILL BOOKS
New York

CONTENTS

I hunted other dinosaurs for my dinner.

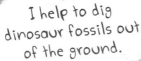

I help to dig dinosaur fossils out of the ground.

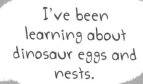

I've been learning about dinosaur eggs and nests.

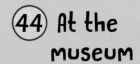

What are dinosaurs?

Dinosaurs are ancient land-dwelling reptiles that once roamed Earth. They died out millions of years ago, but we can learn about them from the traces they left behind.

The word dinosaur means "terrible lizard".

I was one of the first ever dinosaurs.

Herrerasaurus

We don't know exactly what DINOSAURS looked like or what COLORS they were.

Over 800 different types of dinosaurs have been discovered so far.

6

What's in a name?

Dinosaurs are often named after how they look, where they were found, or who found them. *Herrerasaurus* was named after goat herder Victorino Herrera, who first found this dinosaur in Argentina in 1959.

Many dinosaurs had scaly skin. Some, though, had feathers.

Long neck reached leaves and fruits of tall trees

I CAN... SAY THE LONGEST NAME

The longest dinosaur name is... *Micropachycephalosaurus* meaning, "tiny, thick-headed lizard"! Practice saying the name to impress your friends. It should sound like...

AMPELOSAURUS

mike-row-pak-ee-keff-ah-loh-sore-us

Ampelosaurus was as long as two buses!

7

The first dinosaurs

These amazing creatures are thought to be have lived over 230 million years ago. Most early dinosaurs moved around on two legs.

Standing tall

Plateosaurus was a plant eater that could stand on its back legs to reach leaves way up high.

Strong teeth ground up leaves

PLATEOSAURUS

Small and speedy

Eoraptor was a small but fast two-legged dinosaur. It was about 3 feet (1 m) long and weighed about 22 pounds (10 kg) – about the same as a small dog.

EORAPTOR

Good eyesight helped me spot small lizards to eat.

My mouth was filled with lots of saw-shaped teeth for tearing meat.

COELOPHYSIS

I CAN... MAKE A BALANCING DINOSAUR

Draw, color in, and cut out a dinosaur body from half of a paper plate. Use the other half to make the head, neck and tail. Try clipping on two clothespins as legs in different places along the base. Does your dino balance or topple over?

Group hunter

Coelophysis could grow to be about as tall as you. This early dinosaur lived and hunted in large groups.

Dinosaur skeletons are really rare. People were amazed when 100 Coelophysis skeletons were found all together in the United States in 1947.

9

When did dinosaurs live?

Dinosaurs lived on Earth between 235 and 66 million years ago in a time known as the Age of Dinosaurs. This is split into three parts, called the Triassic, Jurassic, and Cretaceous periods.

Humans weren't alive in dinosaur times, but other animals such as insects, fish, lizards, and crocodiles were.

Jurassic

This middle time period was between 200 and 145 million years ago.

Triassic

Dinosaurs first appeared on Earth in Triassic times, between 250 and 200 million years ago.

The first dinosaurs appear. They are small two-legged meat eaters and larger plant eaters.

Apatosaurus

No single type of dinosaur lived throughout the Age of Dinosaurs. Many different kinds came and went.

Procompsognathus

10

Pangaea slowly broke up into smaller chunks of land

One big home

When dinosaurs first lived, all of the land on Earth was clumped together in one big mass called Pangaea. Over time, the land drifted apart, taking dinosaurs to different parts of the planet.

cretaceous

Lots of dinosaurs lived in Jurassic times, including the gigantic plant-eating sauropods.

Huge meat- eaters and large armored plant eaters roamed Earth in the Cretaceous Period.

spinosaurus

I CAN... BUILD A DINOSAUR SKELETON

Build a dinosaur skeleton using dried pasta, a piece of card stock, and some glue. Use penne and other pasta shapes to form the bones of your skeleton. Why not write your dinosaur's name on the card stock as well?

The Cretaceous Period, between 145 and 66 million years ago, was the height of the Age of Dinosaurs.

Shapes and sizes

Dinosaurs came in all kinds of shapes and sizes. Some weighed as much as ten elephants while others were smaller than a chicken.

I ate up to 900 pounds (408 kg) of food every day.

Some of Brachiosaurus's neck bones were 3.3 feet (1 m) long. Yours are about 1.2 inches (3 cm) long.

Speedy **Gallimimus** was a little taller than a tall adult man

Compsognathus was a little meat eater a bit smaller than a turkey

Minmi was a small armored plant eater

Gigantosaurus

A big head and long tail helped make this **massive meat eater** up to 40 feet (12.5 m) long

12

To pump blood around its huge body, *Brachiosaurus*'s heart was probably the size of a trash can.

I CAN... WORK OUT THE WEIGHT

Weigh yourself and then use a calculator or get an adult to help you work out:

1 How many times your weight equals the daily food of a *Brachiosaurus*?

2 How many of you would weigh as much as a *Giganotosaurus*?

3 How many 9-pound (4 kg) *Compsognathus* dinosaurs weigh as much as you?

An adult *Giganotosaurus* could weigh 14.3 tons (13 tonnes). That's more than two elephants!

Brachiosaurus

Great grazers

The prehistoric world was packed with plants, from tall trees to lush bushes and ferns. More than half of all known dinosaur species were plant eaters, munching on plants all day long to survive.

Huge Stegosaurus had a tiny brain – about the size of a walnut!

Slow and strong

Stegosaurus was built like a tank. It weighed up to 4 tons (3.5 tonnes) and moved slowly, eating mostly twigs and leaves.

Bony plates made this dino look bigger and helped it attract a mate

stegosaurus

Beaky mouth pulled up tough plants

Tail spikes helped defend against attackers

14

Spiky thumb

Iguanodon could walk on four legs, but rise up on two to reach taller bushes and trees.

Iguanodon

Thumb spike used for defense and to grab food

Lawn mower mouth

Nigersaurus's mouth contained up to 500 teeth. These cut and chewed up small plants a bit like a lawn mower.

Nigersaurus grew a new set of teeth every few weeks as they wore away quickly.

Nigersaurus

15

Meet the meat eaters

Many dinosaurs hunted other creatures. Some relied on speed and quick reactions to catch creatures. Others used their big size and brute strength.

Troodon was smart, with a big brain for its size

Troodon

Spinosaurus

My large eyes faced forward and could spot small moving creatures even in forest shadows.

SPINOSAURUS was **bigger than** *T. REX!*

Allosaurus stood up to 16 feet (5 m) tall. It hunted Stegosaurus and other slow-moving plant eaters.

ALLOSAURUS

Strong jaws could grip with lots of force

An Allosaurus poop was found that measured 5 feet (1.5 m) long!

I CAN... NAME FIVE CARNIVORES

Meat-eating dinosaurs are called carnivores and plant eaters are called herbivores. Can you think of five carnivores and five herbivores that are around today?

Spinosaurus

Longer than a school bus, this big beast liked hunting in water. It gobbled up huge fish, spearing them with its long jaws full of sharp teeth.

Super-sized sauropods

These dinosaurs were huge plant eaters. They all had long tails to balance out the long necks that they needed to reach plants way up high.

Argentinosaurus had footprints that were more than 5 feet (1.5 m) long!

Argentinosaurus

Heavyweight champion

Argentinosaurus was 115 feet (35 m) long. It weighed about 77 tons (70 tonnes), more than five times the size of *T. rex*.

Diplodocus's long tail was more than half the total length of its body

APATOSAURUS had to eat 900 pounds (400 kg) of food a day to survive.

DIPLODOCUS

Spiny plant eater

Diplodocus was an 85-foot-long (26 m) dinosaur weighing about 22 tons (20 tonnes). It used its peg-shaped teeth to strip leaves off of branches.

I could swing my tail and crack it like a whip to make a loud noise.

I CAN... COMPARE DINOSAUR LENGTHS

Measure the height of one of your friends. Then work out how many of them lying down end to end it would take to be as long as *Argentinosaurus*.

Stomach with stones

APATOSAURUS

Stony stomach

Apatosaurus didn't chew its food but instead swallowed it whole. Like many plant eaters, it also ate large stones that stayed in its stomach and helped grind the food down.

19

Teeth and claws

Dinosaur experts love looking at teeth and claws. These things help to tell us a lot about how dinosaurs lived and the sorts of things they liked to eat.

Plateosaurus

Types of teeth

Dino teeth were well matched to the different sorts of food that dinosaurs ate.

Therizinosaurus was a crazy-looking plant eater that may have been up to 23 feet (7 m) tall!

Therizinosaurus

My teeth were leaf-shaped with jagged edges that stripped the leaves off branches.

Giganotosaurus

I had lots of long, super-sharp teeth used to tear meat.

Gallimimus

My mouth was like a bird's beak – good for pecking at seeds, worms, and bugs.

DEINONYCHUS

I'm a meat eater and my name means "terrible claw" because I have a large curved claw on each foot.

Razor claws

Claws on dinosaurs' hands and feet were used for attack, defense, and to gather food.

Giant curved claw →

Sharp claws cut through plants and tore bark from trees

Therizinosaurus had huge **slashing claws** on its hands up to 3 feet (1 m) in length!

I CAN... CREATE CRAZY DINOSAURS

Draw one half of a dino on the top half of a piece of paper. Make it look as crazy as you like. Fold the paper over so that almost all of your drawing is hidden. Then get a friend to complete the creature. Open the paper to see the finished result.

Horns and armor

Some plant-eating dinosaurs were slow and heavy and couldn't run away from predators. Luckily, they were protected by heavy armor, and some had long horns or clubs too.

Ankylosaurus had armor so thick that an attacker could break its teeth trying to bite through it!

Club of solid bone weighed as much as 15 bricks

Ankylosaurus

Huge bony frill could be raised to make it look even bigger

The two main horns grew up to 3 feet (1 m) long

Triceratops

Three-horned face

Triceratops was enormous – up to 30 feet (9 m) long and 10 feet (3 m) high. A thick, scaly skin and three horns helped protect it from attack.

Ankylosaurus could swing its tail like a giant hammer to bash dinosaurs trying to attack it.

Bonehead

With a big bony dome on its head and a crown of short spikes, *Pachycephalosaurus* butted away predators or rivals.

Skull was 10 inches (25 cm) thick

Triceratops had one of the biggest dinosaur heads – almost a third of its body length.

Pachycephalosaurus

Bony plates provided protection

I CAN... MAKE A TRICERATOPS MASK

Cut one third off a paper plate as shown. Carefully cut out two eyeholes and two small holes at the sides. Next, take some card stock and cut out three horn shapes and a nose and stick to your plate. Color your mask and attach some ribbon or elastic to tie it to your head.

23

Nests and eggs

Dinosaurs hatched from eggs, just like birds and crocodiles today. The smallest dinosaur eggs were just 0.7 inch (1.8 cm) long but others were up to 23.6 inches (60 cm) in length.

Dinosaurs laid big clutches of eggs but only a few survived to become adults. Most were eaten by predators.

Good parents

Troodon parents half buried their eggs in mud in ring-shaped nests. They then sat over the eggs to keep them warm until they hatched.

Troodon

Teardrop-shaped eggs

Inside each egg, a baby dinosaur is forming

Covered up

Some dinosaurs covered their eggs with mounds of twigs and leaves. As the mound rotted, it gave off heat, warming the eggs.

Edmontosaurus

Edmontosaurus looked after its nest and protected the babies from predators

I CAN... FIND DINOSAUR NAMES

Hidden within each set of jumbled letters is the name of a dinosaur. Can you unscramble the letters to find them?

**sea sours tug
coaster trip
old disco up**

Answers: Stegosaurus; Triceratops; Diplodocus

Egg thieves

Eggs and hatchlings were preyed upon by snakes and other dinosaurs.

The snake may have cracked the egg open before it pounced

25

Dino babies

Most baby dinosaurs had to feed and defend themselves as soon as they hatched. Baby *Maiasaura* were lucky. They had parents who cared for them until they could look after themselves.

Maiasaura grew up fast. By their eighth birthday, they could weigh 2.5 tons (2.3 tonnes)!

Maiasaura means "good mother lizard".

Caring colonies

Plant-eating *Maiasaura* lived together in herds and raised their young in colonies. They brought food to their babies while they were still in the nest.

26

A hatchling was about 15.7 inches (40 cm) long

Protecting their young

Adult *Triceratops* may have protected their young from attack by forming a circle around the youngsters with their heads and horns sticking outward.

A *Maiasaura* mom fed babies fruit and leafy twigs

Each nest could contain 40 eggs.

I CAN... GROW UP LIKE A DINOSAUR

Ampelosaurus babies grew from 8.8 pounds (4 kg) at birth to be a huge 17,600 pounds (8,000 kg) – that's 2,000 times bigger! Find out your weight when you were born. Then multiply that figure by 2,000. Bet the answer is heavy!

27

On the move

Just like buffalo or zebras today, some dinosaurs lived in large herds. This helped to protect individuals from attack by fierce meat eaters.

Albertosaurus may have tried to attack young, old, or injured members of the herd

Young *Parasaurolophus* traveled in the middle of the herd for safety

Eyes on the side of the head gave good all-around vision and helped spot predators

Happy herds

We know dinosaurs moved in herds by studying groups of their footprints and skeletons that have all been found in the same place. These *Parasaurolophus* were big dinosaurs that lived in large herds.

Parasaurolophus's huge crest helped it to make a loud sound like a trumpet, perhaps to warn others.

A vast herd of thousands of Centrosaurus skeletons has been found in Canada.

Duck-shaped bill full of teeth ground up tough plants

Young Parasaurolophus walked on **two legs**. As they grew up and got heavier, they often walked on all four.

I CAN... MAKE A DINOSAUR ROAR

Do your best to make a deep, scary roar. Now make a trumpet out of a long cardboard roll and a piece of card stock shaped into a cone at one end. Make a loud trumpeting sound into it. Which is louder?

29

Making tracks

All dinosaurs moved on land, although some also waded through water. We can learn about how they moved from the fossil footprints they left behind.

We measure the space between footprints to figure out if a dinosaur was walking or running.

Fantastic feet

Dinosaur footprints have been found all around the world. Skeletons found nearby help us to identify which dinosaur the footprints belong to.

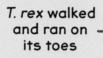

T. rex walked and ran on its toes →

Each of T. rex's footprints are about twice the size of an adult man's →

The biggest dinosaur footprint, found in Australia, belonged to a huge sauropod. It measured 69 inches (175 cm) long and 35.5 inches (90 cm) wide!

Alamosaurus

This heavy dinosaur plodded slowly on its four massive legs

Footprints were up to 31.5 inches (80 cm) long

Struthiomimus was a fast dinosaur, reaching speeds of up to **50 miles (80 km) an hour!**

Powerful legs

I CAN... MAKE DINOSAUR TRACKWAYS

Design a dinosaur foot and ask an adult to cut a sponge to the same shape. Dip your sponge foot into bowls of poster paint and stamp out a trackway of footprints across a large piece of paper.

Struthiomimus looked a bit like a giant ostrich

31

T. rex terror!

Tyrannosaurus rex is one of the most famous and fierce dinosaurs of all. T. rex hunted many other dinosaurs but may also have feasted on dead animals that it found.

Jaws of awe

T. rex's jaws were 4 feet (1.2 m) long – about as long as you are tall! When opened wide, its jaws revealed 60 long, sharp, cone-shaped teeth.

T. rex teenagers got heavier fast. They could add 4.5 pounds (2 kg) to their weight every day.

A T. rex's bite was three times more powerful than a lion's and could crush bone!

Each eye was the size of a grapefruit

Each tooth was 8 inches (20 cm) long – the size of a banana!

A T. rex skeleton found in 1990, called Sue, was sold for $8.3 million dollars!

Short arms with sharp claws

I CAN... MAKE MY OWN T. REX TEETH

Get a large, curved banana and wrap it in thin, white paper using tape. Now imagine 60 of these curved teeth in a giant mouth. Scary stuff!

Powerful legs helped T. rex run up to 12.5 miles (20 km) an hour

T. rex stooped as it moved along so that its head and tail were the same height off the ground.

33

Raptor attack

Not all hunters were huge like *T. rex*. Raptors were usually small, two-legged meat eaters with feathers and vicious claws. Many were smaller than you, but they were fierce hunters.

Tail helped steer when gliding →

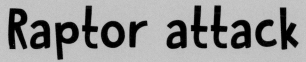

> My name means "speedy thief".

Razor-sharp teeth

Great glider
Chicken-sized *Microraptor* had arms and legs covered in feathers. It used them as wings to glide between branches.

Velociraptor

Fast-moving VELOCIRAPTOR was about the size of a large turkey.

> Velociraptor sometimes hunted in packs to bring down dinosaurs much bigger than themselves.

Hands and feet had sharp, hooked claws

Scary beast

Unusually for raptors, *Utahraptor* was 6.5 feet (2 m) tall. It was the biggest raptor of all.

Utahraptor

Big eyes tracked fast-moving creatures as it hunted

Large curved claw on second toe to attack prey

Utahraptor weighed over 880 pounds (400 kg). That's heavier than a grizzly bear!

I CAN... SPOT THE RAPTOR

Can you end these six dinosaur names correctly using "raptor", "saurus" or "ceratops"?

Tri_____
Ovi_____
Stego _____
Proto _____
Bambi_____
Apato_____

Answers: Triceratops;
Oviraptor;
Stegosaurus;
Protoceratops;
Bambiraptor;
Apatosaurus

35

Up in the air

Soaring high above dinosaurs on the ground, pterosaurs ruled the air. These prehistoric flying reptiles ranged from the size of a small bird to a small airplane.

Pterodactylus
flew over seas to feast on small fish.

I'm one of the smallest pterosaurs, with a wingspan of just 10 inches (25 cm).

Nemicolopterus

Mouth filled with lots of small, cone-shaped teeth

Clawed hands on front wing

Pterodactylus

Large wings measured 20 or 23 feet (6 or 7 m) from tip to tip

Pteranodon

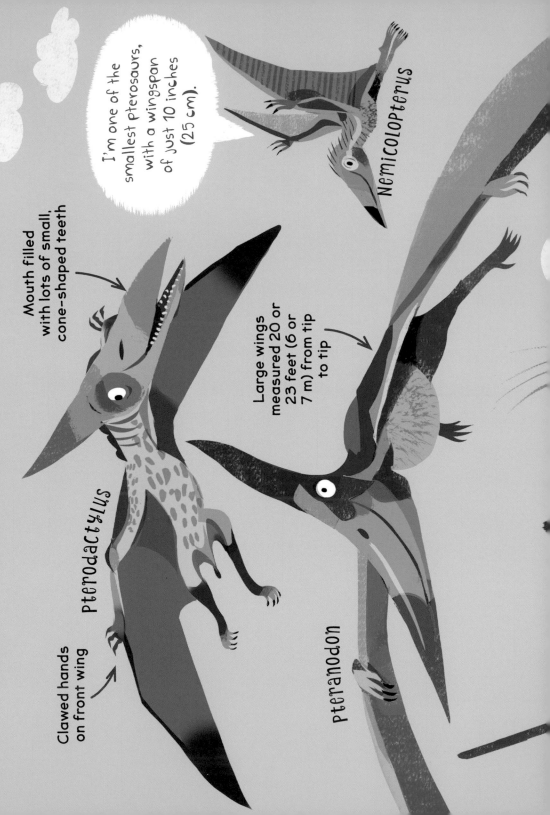

My long, thin beak dipped in water to scoop up fish.

I CAN... DRAW MY OWN PTEROSAUR

Get a big piece of paper and design your own flying reptile. How big would its wings be? What shape would you make its head and tail? What food would it eat? Would it have a crest on its head?

Head crest was twice the length of the body and helped to steer through the air

Quetzalcoatlus

On land, folded wings helped to walk on all fours

Nyctosaurus

Giant glider

The biggest pterosaur of all was *Quetzalcoatlus*. Its wings could measure 36 feet (11 m) from tip to tip. That's four times bigger than the bird with the largest wingspan today, the albatross.

Pterosaurs were the largest creatures ever to fly and many had small, tufty feathers.

37

Under the sea

While the dinosaurs walked the Earth, huge marine reptiles swam in the seas feasting on fish. These reptiles could dive down deep, but all had to come up for air regularly.

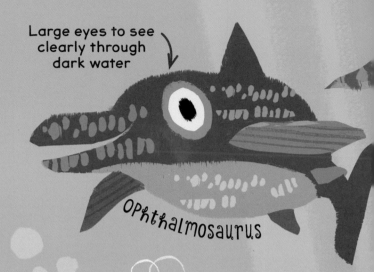

Large eyes to see clearly through dark water

Ophthalmosaurus

Shastasaurus

Long, flexible neck swept through shoals of fish

Shastasaurus was the biggest marine reptile at 69 feet (21 m) long - about the length of three Killer whales.

Elasmosaurus

Four large flippers paddled through the water

Sea turtles, squid, and jellyfish swam in prehistoric oceans and are still around today.

38

Mosasaurus weighed twice as much as an elephant!

MOSASAURUS

Extra rows of teeth helped catch and swallow prey

I CAN... MAKE LOTS OF WORDS

Use the word "OPHTHALMOSAURUS" to create as many new words as you can by rearranging the letters. Each word must be at least two letters long. Use a dictionary to check the spelling of your words.

Huge fins and a good sense of smell made me a fast swimmer and top hunter.

Liopleurodon

A large skull full of sharp teeth gave a powerful bite

39

The end of the dinosaurs

An asteroid streaks across the sky

Dinosaurs lived on Earth until about 66 million years ago when they disappeared. This is what we think happened...

① The last dinosaurs

Around 66 million years ago, dinosaurs were still thriving on land. Big beasts like *Triceratops*, *Ankylosaurus*, and mighty *T. rex* were all still alive.

② Impact!

An asteroid (a large rock from space) struck Earth. It sent huge clouds of dust into the air, blocking out the sun and making Earth much colder and darker than before.

③ Dying out

Earth went through climate change for many years. Lots of plants died out and so did many creatures, including all of the dinosaurs.

Many volcanoes also erupted, adding to the damage

④ Survivors

Some creatures survived including crocodiles, turtles, snakes, and birds. New animals appeared after the dinosaurs, including monkeys, wild cats, and us – humans!

Seeds survived, providing food for birds after the asteroid impact

Fossil clues

Dinosaurs may be gone, but they left behind their remains, which are known as fossils. Most of what we know about these amazing creatures comes from finding fossils.

American George Frandsen has a COLLECTION of 1277 fossilized dinosaur POOPS!

How fossils are made

Fossils take thousands and sometimes millions of years to form. Lying under layers of rock, the dinosaur's skeleton dissolves away. It leaves space that is filled by a stony substance that forms a replica of the dinosaur's bones.

① A **dinosaur** dies. Its soft parts **rot** away and it gets covered in layers of sand or mud that eventually turn to rock.

② The dinosaur's **skeleton** dissolves and is replaced with a stony substance, forming a **fossil**.

A **complete skeleton** is a very rare and **exciting** find.

Trace fossils are things like nests, footprints, and dung left behind by dinosaurs.

Fossils are carefully cut out from the surrounding rock

I CAN... MAKE A FOSSIL

Make dough by mixing 1 cup of salt with 2 cups of flour and about ½ cup of water. Divide it into six pieces and shape them into flattened rounds, like a cookie. Press shells, toy insects, or toy dinosaurs into the dough, remove, and let your fossils dry and harden overnight.

Dinosaur skeletons have to be pieced together, bone by bone, like a jigsaw puzzle.

③ Millions of years later, the rocks have moved or are worn away to reveal the **fossil**.

At the museum

Fancy going face-to-face with real-life dinosaur skeletons? What about seeing full-sized dinosaur models move and roar? There's no better place to go than a dinosaur museum!

Pterosaurs were flying reptiles that lived at the same time as the dinosaurs.

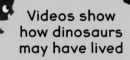

Videos show how dinosaurs may have lived

If you look hard when walking along a beach, you may even find your own fossil!

What we know about dinosaurs often changes as new discoveries are made.

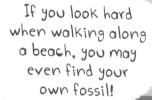

I CAN... MAKE A PREHISTORIC POSTER

Pick a dinosaur, perhaps one from this book, and make your own poster all about it. Draw a large picture of your dinosaur, color it in, and write lots of facts about it in the spaces. Use your school library or ask a teacher to help you learn more.

Wow, that's HUGE!

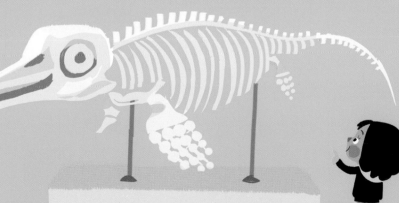

Fossil hunter

Mary Anning (1799–1847) was just 12 years old when she found an ichthyosaur fossil near her home in southern England over 200 years ago. Mary went on to discover lots of other fossils during her lifetime.

Glossary

Armor

A strong, hard covering that protects a creature from harm.

Asteroid

A chunk of rock in space that travels around the sun. Some asteroids crash into planets like Earth.

Climate change

When the general weather patterns around the world alter greatly.

Dissolves

When a substance disappears, often through being mixed with water.

Flexible

Something that can bend easily without breaking.

Fossil

The remains of plants and creatures, including dinosaurs, that lived a long time ago. Fossils are often found preserved in rock.

Hatchlings

Very young creatures that have just hatched out of their eggs.

Herd

A large group of animals that live together.

Jaws

The bony parts of any animal's head that hold their teeth.

Predators

Creatures, including dinosaurs like *T. rex*, that hunt and kill other creatures for food.

Prehistoric

Times before anything was written down. This period stretches back millions of years.

Prey

Creatures that are hunted and eaten by others.

Pterosaur

A flying reptile from dinosaur times.

Replica

A copy of something that looks very similar to the original.

Reptile

A cold-blooded animal that usually has dry, scaly skin and uses the heat of the sun to keep its blood warm.

Sauropod

A type of giant plant-eating dinosaur that moved on four legs and had a long neck and tail.

Skeleton

The framework of bones that supports an animal's body.

Trackway

A path or trail formed by lots of animals' footprints all following the same route.

Say my name

Dinosaur names can be hard to pronounce.
Use this handy guide to learn to say their names.

Dinosaurs

Alamosaurus	A-lam-oh-SORE-us	Maiasaura	my-a-SORE-a
Allosaurus	AL-oh-SORE-us	Microcephalosaurus	MI-kro-sef-alo-SORE-us
Ampelosaurus	am-PEL-oh-SORE-us	Microraptor	MY-crow-RAP-tor
Ankylosaurus	an-kee-lo-SORE-us	Minmi	min-mee
Apatosaurus	a-PAT-oh-SORE-us	Nigersaurus	nai-ja-SORE-us
Argentinosaurus	ar-jen-TEEN-oh-SORE-us	Pachycephalosaurus	pak-ee-sef-alo-SORE-us
Brachiosaurus	BRAK-ee-oh-SORE-us	Parasaurolophus	para-sore-ROL-oh-fus
Coelophysis	see-loh-FIE-sis	Plateosaurus	pla-tee-oh-SORE-us
Compsognathus	komp-sog-NATH-us	Spinosaurus	SPY-noh-SORE-us
Deinonychus	di-NON-ee-kus	Stegosaurus	STEG-oh-SORE-us
Diplodocus	dip-lo-DOKE-us	Struthiomimus	STREW-theo-MY-mus
Edmontosaurus	ed-MON-toe-SORE-us	Tyrannosaurus rex	tie-RAN-oh-sore-us rex
Eoraptor	EE-oh-RAP-tor	Therizinosaurus	thera-ZINA-SORE-us
Gallimimus	gal-lee-MY-mus	Triceratops	tri-SERRA-tops
Giganotosaurus	jig-ano-toe-SAW-rus	Troodon	TRUE-oh-don
Herrerasaurus	heh-RARE-ra-SORE-us	Utahraptor	U-ta-RAP-tor
Iguanodon	ig-WAH-noh-don	Velociraptor	ve-LOSS-ee-RAP-tor

Pterosaurs

Nemicolopterus	NEM-ee-kol-OPT-er-us
Nyctosaurus	NIC-to-SORE-us
Pteranodon	te-RAN-oh-don
Pterodactylus	terra-DACT-aluss
Quetzalcoatlus	ket-zal-KWAT-luss

Marine reptiles

Elasmosaurus	el-lazz-mo-SORE-us
Liopleurodon	LIE-oh-PLUR-a-don
Mosasaurus	moe-za-SORE-us
Ophthalmosaurus	op-THAL-mo-SORE-us
Shastasaurus	SHAZ-ta-SORE-us